Birdwatching
in Wartime

Books by Jeffrey Thomson

Poetry

The Halo Brace
The Country of Lost Sons
Renovation
Birdwatching in Wartime

As Editor

From the Fishhouse: An Anthology of Poems that Sing, Rhyme, Resound,
Syncopate, Alliterate, and Just Plain Sound Great

Birdwatching in Wartime

poems by Jeffrey Thomson

Carnegie Mellon University Press
Pittsburgh 2009

Acknowledgments

These poems have appeared, sometimes in different versions, in the following publications and online archives:

32 Poems: fabulous ones (reprinted on *Verse Daily* and *From the Fishouse*)
Drunken Boat: Stalin on Stage
The Café Review: Landscape with Flooded Forest & American Pastoral
Cimarron Review: Landscape with Swelling and Hives
The Fourth River: Landscape with Pigeons and the Tree of Heaven
From the Fishouse: Ars Poetica with Pain, fabulous ones, innumerable ones
    & those that have just broken a flower vase
Ginger Hill: Twin
Ginko Tree Review: Birdwatching in Wartime
Image: Underwhelmed & Quo Vadis?
Indiana Review: innumerable ones (reprinted on *From the Fishouse*)
Quarterly West: Landscape with Urban Elephants & Amazon Parable
    (reprinted on *Verse Daily*)
Sea Stories: those that are not included in this classification
Southern Indiana Review: mermaids & those drawn with a very fine camel's
    hair brush
Sycamore Review: those that belong to the emperor

Celestial Emporium of Benevolent Knowledge was published as a chapbook by
    RopeWalk Press, 2007.
Blind Desire appeared as a limited edition art book printed in English and Braille
    with companion photographs by Dennis Marsico produced by Dionysus
    Press, 2005.
"Praise for my Nation of Meat and Phonemes" is from *Biographia: poesía completa,*
    1958-1984. (Anthropos, 1986) © Felix Grande.

Book design: Nancy Lee

The National Endowment for the Arts, the Pennsylvania Council on the Arts,
the Maine Arts Commission, Chatham College, and the University of Maine
Farmington provided support for the time during which this book was written.

Publication of this book is made possible by a grant from
the Pennsylvania Council on the Arts.

PENNSYLVANIA
COUNCIL
ON THE
ARTS

Library of Congress Control Number 2008941545
ISBN 13: 978-0-88748-511-4 Pbk.

10 9 8 7 6 5 4 3 2 1

Contents

This book is what it is due to the help of many people. Specifically, Terrance Hayes, Wes McNair, Penelope Pelizzon, Adrian Blevins, Robert Hass, Chad Davidson, Terri Witek, and Christian Barter helped me immeasurably with these poems. Additional thanks are due to Jerry Costanzo and Cynthia Lamb for their continued support, and to Ron Mitchell, who didn't get thanked the last time. Muchas gracias para todos a Luis Torres: Pura vida, amigo. In fact, thanks to all my guides and teachers: Dolly and Moises, Solomon, Michi, and Franklin. Thanks to Drew Barton, Lynne Bruckner, Pat Demase, and Michael Shriberg for coming with me; to my parents and sister for helping while I was gone; and to Julian and Jennifer Anne for letting me go.

For Jennifer and Julian,
mi cielo, mi alma, mi vida

Praise for my Nation of Meat and Phonemes

translated from the Spanish of Félix Grande

Those apathetic few who eat the bread
of dialect and wear it as ornament, armor
or blackmail suffer me as a furious reflection:
I have called patria *only you and language.*

Those who dedicate hymns and medals and love
to the raven of war and never to the dove
of lust look grudgingly upon my bed:
I have called patria *only you and the language*

of brotherhood and civil honor:
no one feels it, no one radiates it,
if this tongue is channeled into slang
and in your body the marvelous flame smothers.

Celebrated like a god, the hand's fire
feels for the words a mighty respect:
only thus can the transient be our brother
and matter and the world our friend.

The meat that has taught me most deeply knows:
the teaching language is an ancient lexicon:
time is the embrace of a man and a woman,
the universe is a formidable word.

I

Landscape with Swelling and Hives

> *And here, or there. . . . No. Should we have stayed at home,*
> *wherever that may be?*
>
> —Elizabeth Bishop

When the *tsawaim* swam from the deadfall across the path
    (a moss-grown nurse log
hosting a thrumming mess of life in its rain-woven campus),
    when those wasps
stapled my back and sides and face and sent me at a run down
    the piebald path,
when the rainforest trembled, fishtail palms kicking their fins
    in the green welter
beneath the canopy, when the splotches flushed across my arms,
    my neck, my sweat-licked face,
when the diaspora of venom wrote a question across my back
    in hot letters that left me
cold and shaking and desperately needing to piss, I had no sense,
    stunned and numb,
that my throat might close, not even when my tongue went dumb
    like a river
fat with flood, no thought that the last sight I'd see would be
    a green shriek
of light carried through the trees. The wasps stung for nothing
    I had done;
the others passed that path before me, the chill washed out
    in sweat,
and the landscape tumbled back to form, but, hours out,
    perhaps
I should have made my peace, prepared myself among the *pitchurina*
    and *pucahuasca*
and waited for the infinite to break through the canopy in a spray
    of green-gone-gold.
In the end, nothing came of this. My throat stayed open and
    the canopy closed.
It's the distance out from camp—the gas lamps lit and tented
    in the shifting dark,
the house macaw patrolling the piered walkways, little chevrons
    flashing on his shoulders—
that makes it menacing. Yes, it would have been a pity not to have seen
    the spattered sun
scribbled down to nothing more than matchlight on army ants
    engraving leaf litter,

the cuneiform of tapir prints in the mud of that flat-banked stream,
      not to have seen
the wattled jacana scrawl across water lilies with her vast, forked feet,
      a pity
never to have taken piranha from the river and watched them slap
      their gibberish
across the bottom of the boat, yes, a pity never to have read the remains
      of a saddleback tamarin
(a slur of fur and black fingers) as the fact of a jaguar in the night,
      yes, a pity, yes,
but what now's the answer to that question written across my skin?

Landscape with Flooded Forest

Amazonia, January 2004

1.

When the horizon rises up around the shoulders of the trees
and fish fly through branches in flocks of scale

and saucer eyes, and the bird-hunters billboard webs
across the water in the shrubby canopy

of ceiba and cercropia, the strangler fig splayed out
in a skeletal fan and colonnades of kapok,

when the white sun soon finishes off the dawn
and tree boas sleep tentacled above the water

across a fan of leaves to avoid the crush of noon,

2.

when a wire-tailed manakin flames
through the middle-story treetops and pink dolphins

slalom through the sunken trunks
to hunt tambaqui that feed on fallen fruit,

tiny coconuts of summer's plenty,

when the seeping tannin water, deep as steeped tea,
consumes the edges of the trees

and we float above a forest doubled in the water
(a clicking symphony of fish trickles

up through our wooden canoe),

the water will be halfway up the sky
and not yet finished rising.

3.

At night, beneath ficus trunks that arch and plunge
in gothic tangles, the bang and stammer

of the tree frogs' need orchestrates desire in the forest.
Quarter-sized they come gluey off the mimosa,

eyes red as blood blisters

beneath our lights as the golden foil of caiman eyeshine
along the banks balances

4.

the smear of stars across the sky.

5.

Tarantulas that hunt fish—the black goliath and the Peruvian
pinktoe—strike out across the water as we pass

and a blue-crowned trogon

sits stunned and blinking beneath our headlamps.
We raise the landscape into meaning and return it

damaged in our wake—the slap

of water off the paddles, the sweep and beam of lights
tunneling through the dark.

Trauma is what we carry and the world retires from us
in radiating waves, but (*recall it now!*)

6.

the frogs, they deafened us that night.

7.

Horned screamers play a quartet across the high-ground
grass, as we haul our canoe through the canopy

branch by branch

like boat-building simians. This ancient bird
we're searching for, the hoatzin,

in the wet savannah remnants, croaks and heaves—
a heavy smoker's wheeze—

8.

beneath the deadwood overhead, a blue-faced, mohawked relic
(a claw-winged, almost *archaeopteryx*)

lizard-hops and pants trying to stay cool. We eat and wait
and watch the heat pile clouds up the sky.

Rain threatens its black opera as we slip out
through the trees writing down birds for inscrutable lists.

9.

Anis and oropendulas crisscross the open canopy
where three rivers seam together, kingfishers

chatter, skimming low and loud above the russet water,

and at our feet jerk piranha, red-bellied as rage.
Morpho butterflies spatter the streaked light sapphire.

Soaked with birdcall and blue fluttering, the trees
fill with water and the swift kick of fins.

The air charged with all that hasn't happened yet,
the water with all that has—

10.

the toucan that will be taken from a branch and guzzled
to bloody feathers and the hard beak tip

by a harpy eagle.
Piranhas that disassembled a swimming sloth.

Lakes drain out of the basin leaving a shoreline scoured.
Banks reappear in a maze of mud.

The season of want approaches and recedes. The sunlight
and the heat, and, soon,

the water giving way.

Birdwatching in Wartime

The rain comes and the sound
of water hitting water raises
an ovation, the canal pocky
with applause. We move up river,
hoods up, heads down, the boat
ottering through the trees. When
sunlight breaks free and disrobes
in the canopy we see the heron—
a tiger—striped and striated
and thick on a snag. She rolls
her shoulders, wings out to catch
the light, rainforest backlit
behind her, looming up like praise.

At sunset a *guanacaste*, a single
sculpted cone of flooded forest
rising from water licked with
the last light, currents of lavender
and ginger drawing through
the slough, water and a tree,
solitary. Then a multitude
of birds, flamingo gawky but
a deeper red, came dropping in
along the water to rise and cup
the wind and awkward fall into
branches against a failing sky.
All night, scarlet ibis painted
that tree, drop by unbearable drop.

In the early dawn, a trogon stoic
as a general in the ficus and great
green macaws in the crowns
of wild almonds—metallic calls,
little soldiers with their chevroned
shoulders. They storm through
the canopy raining almond shells
like shrapnel on the forest floor.
Dawn marshals above the trees
as the light assembles on their tops,
marches down the canopy. How

easily it turns, how quickly words
slip, like knives into rinds. My hushed
footsteps through leaflitter,
my DEET-numb lips. The guides
have left us, sick from metaphor,
scopes up on their shoulders
like rifles. They have long since felt
a change in the weather and step
awkwardly away through shin-deep
mud and fishtail palms, calling
after toucans: *Dios-te-dé, Dios-te-dé!*
In their minds they are already laughing
and smoking beneath the lean-to
as the rain gallops down around them.

Twin

The Psi function for the entire system would express this by having in
it the living and the dead cat (pardon the expression) mixed or smeared
out in equal parts.
       —E. Schrödinger
       "Die gegenwartige Situation in der Quantenmechanik"

Fall has finally come in a torrent
that tears leaves from the locust—
glitter mucking up the gutter,
choking the storm sewer, water
backing up, bowed with oil and filmy—
and, no, what it makes me think of
is not love dying, the glorious bronze
rage and ruin of the last days, and
not my own age yammering in the dark
as it loses control of its bladder again
and the piss rains out on the mat
before the toilet golden as shame, no,
not all that, but strangely enough,
a cat, a particular cat locked in a box,
forced to live its life stalking corners,
unaware of the isotope's decay hanging
fire in that space like a bare bulb,
the one that will split its life in two (two
halves unhalved and parallel): one cautious,
alive and aware, green foil of eyeshine,
the other flat and black as a burn
on the floor. They exist together,
the carcass and the stalking silhouette,
witched together by possibility's spell.
But I'm afraid it's all just metaphor,
quantum reflection in the mirror of desire.
Not the cat alive *or* dead, but both
at once: love and its failure, metaphor
and madness, youth and age with
its orchestra of sighs, the leaves
streaming through the storm-rich dark
and the mess they cause in the gutter.
Metaphor strokes the cat and buries it,
slides out from beneath the last daylight,
straightens her skirt and smoothes her
pink-streaked hair. Metaphor turns the air

to viognier and buys a round for the house—
she's generous that way. Metaphor
fucks a guy she finds in the bathroom,
makes him a poet. Metaphor stalks
through the night, painting the air
with a waste of _____ that makes even
bridges beautiful. She wakes in the morning
without regret, but Metaphor doesn't talk
about her twin brother, locked away
in the hospital, pacing an ellipse
into the carpet beneath the single bulb
always on in that windowless room.

American Pastoral

First, there's the rank stupidity
of their mucilaginous mouths,
their wide rolling eyes

that look up as you pass (your dog
at your heels) like white Jell-o
molds bouncing on a bumped table

where the burgers and hot dogs
line up eager as children
before the condiments and cheese,

flaccid sheaves of iceberg lettuce,
and the watermelon smiles
echo the cisterns of bunting

that hang from the slatted porch
in the sunlight. Chewy automatons,
but there's a sentimentality to the way

they spread themselves across
the field, the shattered yin-yang
of their hides, the way they clump

together beneath the thin, stripped
maples, their square butts ripe
with flies. The fields flow over

the hill and beyond, the blue sky
speckled with the white froth
of the clouds and the cows

plotz and shuffle their thickness
down to the farmer who has moved
across this field on his quad-runner,

the fenders flared and startled
with mud, and it is no longer
the century you were imagining.

The farmer has his laptop out
and enters a herd of data
into the machine, driving it

through his Wi-Fi to the small barn
of a spreadsheet, taming it the way
his cows are tame, microchip ear-tags
dangling like the last leaves in autumn.

Landscape with Urban Elephants

*No one knows exactly how many elephants
there are in Bangkok.*

— PBS

Up from the dumps and the red hollows
where water wells from the bottle-speckled mud,

up from the scrub and cracked palms, up from the can-fires
into the dazzle and slither of traffic muscling

around these boulders of hide and waddle,
up from a distant bliss of tree fern and orchid,

from mahogany and kapok, the elephants come
to the city. Big-shouldered and wattled.

Their slow bop strut up the boulevards,
a repertoire of rolled eights kept by the metronome

of bottlebrush tails syncopated by reflecting tape
patched across their asses. Painting elephants,

dancing elephants, peanut-eating, banana-slinging
elephants, half-smiles and great, gray Walt Whitman eyes

above the bike lights that swing from their trunks.
Traffic swerves around their oil-slick piles of shit.

Beneath it all, a squall of noise, flutter of trunks,
they sing: *platter-foot, big toe, skin of wet burlap.*

They sing: *It don't mean a thing if it ain't got that swing.*
Deep into the night alight with sodium

their back-beat rumbles travel for miles, pacing
a high-hat rhythm the tuk-tuks keep beneath the Skytrain.

They totter off to sleep it off beneath the milk-colored
dawn as their tails keep their own rough time.

II

CELESTIAL EMPORIUM
OF BENEVOLENT KNOWLEDGE:
a Sequence

In "The Analytical Language of John Wilkins,"
Jorge Luis Borges describes a Chinese Encyclopedia, in which
it is written that all plants and animals may be divided into:

1. those that belong to the Emperor

A cat sweeping dawn into the corners
of the City. Pheasants with black heads
and necks squared in crimson that warble
and cluck when tossed grain. Sable antelope
clacking their horns among willow branches
by the river. Trumpet vine, heliotrope, the red
bird of paradise. Flies spinning above sliced
melon. Ten thousand rhododendrons and
the green writhing of dahlias. Globe-eyed carp
among saucers of hyacinth. The dragon
of morning and evening. Gibbons and
the orangutan that haunts the trees beyond
the terrace. Hornbills and buntings.
The raffish pose of the frill-necked lizard.
Mackerel and tuna stacked on ice. Mandrills
like clowns. Three stags and a decomposing body
laid out on a slab. Binturong. Bromeliad.
Clownfish and anemones. Five thousand butterflies
and one lepidopterist. A family of yak.
Tiger lilies with their mouths full of bees.
The clouded leopard that hunts mice and frightens
the horses. Cattle. Roses and the spring litter
of cherry trees. Cattails, irises, the emerald heads
of pintail ducks. Anything the heart desires:
A bat in a cage without a door. Tiny elephants
and the lizards that hunt them. Glass frogs,
their visible hearts hammering through their skin.
Lungfish. Spiders the size of books. A handful
of stones and two eggs of unknown origin.

2. those drawn with a very fine camel's hair brush

It's not what I thought, not matted mohair
shaved from the gamy flank and Mr. Camel,
the inventor, not named for the harelip,
for the split toes, for the godawful smell
and the knees swollen as breadfruit.
Not *ata Allah*—God's gift—with its boat-
rolling gait. Not the ropey tail.
Rather, it's the ox or the goat,
squirrel or pony, *carcasses* abandoned
for the delicacy of a *caress*. Remains
as in affirmation, as in a man stroking
the cheekbones of his telescope's mirror
on the high balcony, the city painted up
around him like the caves at Lascaux,
tinted bulls in ocher and carmine,
the bird-headed man scorched in cinnamon
and the swimming stags. True stars
extinct in the city, the night sky gone
the color of sun-baked asphalt, a welter
of traffic rivering beneath his feet,
he watches a man and a woman undress
each other down the barrel of 3rd Avenue,
their several shadows burned onto the wall
as with the delicacy of a camel's hair brush.

3. those that are trained

The dog behind the fence is a symbol
for desire, for the anywhere-but-here grit
on the teeth found up the endless swerve
of river road high at the end of the valley.
The bent paneling, creased as tar
in the den, where the blue suede
from the small black and white
fills the room and the only channel
on this late is a gospel station
where a preacher mutters and sweats
then gut punches a man whose cancer
has returned, the paneling says something
too about desire as the room
goes gravel-colored with smoke,
the remains of a dimebag on a black
album striped by the full spectrum.
But leave them now, these two boys
who might be you and me, these boys
made up of memory and ash
and smoke, these two boys who have
the TV turned down and *Dark Side*
cranked again and the alarms are
detonating and the bells and the clock
tick-tocks like a damaged heart and
it all seems at once easy and impossible
because the road down valley is the only road
to everywhere as the dog barks and barks
and will never, ever, shut the fuck up.

4. fabulous ones

This poem is brought to you by the letter C.

Cattle egret, Big Bird says, *cetacean*,
the word squeaking like wet whale skin.

Big Bird keeps it real—his thug-life strut.

Do you like giants?
Only the small ones, the boy says.

Chinese catfish, cassava, cassowary.

He's an intellectual, spends his days off
in coffeehouses, crossing and uncrossing
the long orange tubes of his legs, discussing

Chomsky, conditional freedom, and Cervantes

with anyone who will listen. He marches
against the war, a thousand people
at his back, chanting

Catastrophe, cruise missile, children.

Big Bird refuses to fly south for the winter,
puts on his scarf and heads out the door.

You can't fool me, the boy says.
I know Big Bird's not real.
It's just a suit with a little bird inside.

5. mermaids

She comes ashore alone, humping
through the surf like an elephant seal.

Waves slam on the flat sand and the hillside's
afire with Christmas lights swagged

on piled balconies, the beach half-canyoned
by the high-rises ripping up the sky.

Her whiskers drip like piss, six flabby tits
down her chest, but her voice, when

she opens up that clam-can mouth,
comes on like Nina Simone's, gargantuan,

as the sand flies tear at her wrists
bent backwards on the sand. No one

comes out from the condos on the shore—
Tommy Dorsey's on the radio and the news

comes on at five. A corona of gulls tears
at plastic sacks dreadlocked in her hair

as she funnels into the chorus
what might be of *Love Me or Leave Me*

alone on a swollen tongue of beach.
The surprising velocity of dusk as the light fails.

6. stray dogs

gather behind the zoo
  to test the fence
and run the antelope,
  skittish the gazelles,
and scatter the dawning
  flamingos. In the morning
small bleating sheep
  shy from the carcass
of their own, entrails
  running bloody ribbons
along the corn and sawdust
  floor. A pronghorn's
haunch glazed with flies
  half buried in the leaves,
but the dogs are long gone,
  hiding, bramble-tied,
curled in sleep, the day
  rotten with light,
as the sun piles up the sky.

7. those that tremble as if they were mad

Sunlight slits into the mist which lingers
          in the forest, leaves
                    so jittery with the pulse
          of dripping water their shadows
                    tremble on the forest floor

and a hummingbird—a green violet-ear—haunts
          the lilac-blazed path
                    down the Rio Savegre valley
          where in stock ponds trout rib the water
                    with interlocking loops as they rise

towards a late hatch of stonefly.
          The bird's incomprehensible heart
                    hammers up into the rafters
          of its chest as its black tongue wires
                    the blossoms from below,

and what this has to do with knowledge,
          who can say? Madness could be
                    the road down canyon,
          laddered switchbacks testing the gearbox,
                    could be coffee plantations

woven into the cliffside, the crimson *pointillisme*
          of the fruit against
                    the waxy leaves. But benevolence
          must be the oceanic color of the tear
                    that streaks the emerald iridescence,

must be the act of naming
          this bird for the sea—*Colibri thalassinus.*
                    Far from the shore,
          the clouds' surf breaks against the coast
                    of the cordillera far below.

8. those that are *not* included in this classification

Just as Don Quixote,
crumpled as laundry
and laid out across

the Spanish *paisaje*,
pukes up into the face
of Sancho Panza,

and Sancho, hovering
and concerned for his
oafish, wounded lord,

follows suit and pukes down
into the face of the man
who promised him

a garden ripe with cockatoos
and the fleshy erotics
of the seabreeze,

so the black tulips
stunned with carmine or
a gaudy wisp of violet rip

through the leaf-litter, swing
and knock against each other
like mallets. It's spring

and the new sun, the lawn
paved with fat platters
of magnolia blossoms.

The wind rises and shreds
Sancho's island of sunlight
and fog, the galloping

surf of the rough, windward coast
where the name of every lost creature
gets written on pages of air,

where the dodo chuckles and grunts,
where the ivory-billed woodpecker
jackhammers long-leaf pine,

and dusky seaside sparrows
metronome marsh grass down
the scoured, dune-heavy shore.

9. embalmed ones

Take the body into the tent,
wash it with palm wine
and rinse in the water of the Nile.

> *Rats and cats sacked*
> *in freeze-dried packs.*

Cut into the left side, always left,
and gather all organs save
the heart—it will be needed.

> *Sliced sections of a human head*
> *suspended in green fluid.*

With bronze hooks inserted
up the sinuses and through
the ethmoid bone, a twist of

> *A Gobi bear, a camel fetus, that two-headed*
> *dog with its permanent snarl,*

the wrist is all it takes to extract
the brains. Rub the body with natron.
Stuff with sawdust, leaves and linen—

> *and all the species*
> *in the genus* Arctocephalus.

it can be made quite lifelike.
After forty days, wash again with wine
and myrrh. Wrap in linen, alternating

> *Baboons, birds, and crocodiles.*
> *Sacred bulls in their own cemetery at Sakkara.*

coats of resin. A priest will perform
the rites to Open the Mouth. Now
the body can eat and drink, smell

Hunger preserved in a collection
of sheep stomachs,

the flowers of the afterlife, taste the names
of the fruits of the dead. The heart remains
inside waiting for its counter weight—

the last Tasmanian wolf
dead in a Hobart zoo.

10. suckling pigs

This encyclopedia of articulate nothing,
taxonomy of damage, library of sand.
Manuscript of clouds, archipelago of crabs
in a wash of seafoam. I could write anything—
a pack of pigs sucking at the blank canvas
of the sow's belly—and you'd believe it.

11. others

The rainbow hits the water hard,
           a spray of color almost physical—
     wind rich and horizontal
           from the west—rain tearing
       gnarled waves, coconut froth
and ratty, wet raffia in the soup.

The ocean's the conclusion
           to the clumsy whisper of names
     we read onto the land—hummock, tussock,
           beach, spit, strand. No words
       for the choppy shove of the waves,
the ache they leave on the sand slipping away.

Lianas, waree palm, mahogany.
           The estuary humming with the tongues
     of many rivers—*Chirripo, Sierpe, Suerte*—
           as *rana con* blue jeans,
       the blue jeans frog (*Dendrobates pumilio*),
thumbnail small in the tannin muck

and fishtail palm, trills its delicate Morse.
           All that language tunneling into
     the steaming earth as the sun returns,
           awkward somehow, this business.
       We live in the words we use,
says Wittgenstein, so what to make

of the parataxis of genus and species—
           the Latin running underneath it all,
     electric life of a dead language
           translated here to the tri-color of exile?
       A large brunette bird whistles
and pops as it hunts in the crown of palms.

In English it's Montezuma's Oropendula
           and the Latin's pure gold: *Psarocolius montezuma.*
     At night green sea turtles return
           to nest on this eponymous coast,
       heads down in the wracked sand, laboring
with their winged, inarticulate hands.

Chelonia mydas, their owlish eyes tear up
      in the desiccate air. Sea oats
toss their blond hair. They see little
      beyond sand tented with driftwood
but gasp with beaked mouths as if drowning
in the incomprehensible surf of the wind.

12. innumerable ones

How to count? Begin with one, or $n + 1$
where n is the number of ants in a colony,
and 1 is you looking over your own shoulder,
looking into the earth, driving a stick down
into the mound like a gifted chimp, pulling it out
to count the inscrutable bodies, huge-headed
warriors sawing the wood. Where n is bacteria
and 1 is your colon, the wealth of E. *coli*
colonizing and shifting upriver, where n
is the burger you ate yesterday and 1 is you
heaving into the sink and falling back
wracked with fever. Where n is brine shrimp
and 1 the stink they make on a hot day,
the light above the Great Salt Lake gone flat
and gauzy. Where n is the caribou cresting
across the Porcupine in the Yukon and n^2
the mosquitoes that blind them—eyes jammy
with crushed bodies—and drive them mad.
Where 1 is the Cessna and the rifle,
where 1 is the bullet and the carcass
resting on the tundra's mossy sponge.

13. those that have just broken a flower vase

Because some birds land only to nest,
because they travel through the canyon's
half-light like science fiction standards,
the swerve and veer through a dangerous chute,
because down valley the landscape fades
to a geometric test of wills—algebraic
agriculture arguing with the river's
floodplain calculus—because the clouds
branch and froth in blossom above
the Allegheny Mountains, because
these peaks have been lifted up
and torn down three times, because
exhaustion writes its name in deer trails
across the smoky hillsides in midwinter,
because beauty walks hand in hand
with grief, because it's the only time
she'll ever see one, I'll talk about
the collared swift that died in flight
(family name *Apodidae*—without feet)
and landed in my neighbor's pachysandra.
The picture window rang where
it smacked the glass. Framed in the casement,
her husband drops to his knees in the March-wet
earth, a stroke blooming up the branches
in his head. At least that is how I choose
to imagine it—the gelling of the narrative
around the low tone of rung glass,
the warm carcass of the bird splayed
in the elegant green of the new shoots,
his dead-arm slump as the cat, startled, drops
from the pie chest and knocks a bud vase
from its place. So, as she turns to find
the door, she sees them both there
suspended in midair with the grace
of everything about to shatter.

14. those that look like flies from a distance

Start simply—
                  the dead snag filled
with white herons near Caño Blanco,
the muscular press of clouds above,
the colonnade a plane slices into
and the sudden smallness of the plane
seen from the ground, farmers
looking up from their fields of aloe,
the plants like rows of jade octopi
and the pearl buttons on their shirts
iridescent as flies. A bottle hive
of paper wasps hanging from
the middle story treetops along
the road to San Isidro becomes
the eye of a gazelle gone gauzy and fly-
charmed on the hot savannah below
a hillside glossy with wildebeest.
Pink dolphins roiling blackwater
as they herd tucunare within the flooded
forest turn to squadrons of toucans
streaming through back-lit kapoks,
long-tendriled lianas, the silver-edged
leaves of the winter's bark trees
school in the wet air like herring.
Plankton bloom in the cold upwelling
of the Chukchi Sea. Shrimp feed
so delicately on the plankton
and sand eels gorge on the shrimp.
I close the book where I have been writing
all day; the unused pages fall whitely
over the City. *What have you learned?*
The words churn, a mob of bitterns
thrash about the corpse of a marten,
hagfish writhe on a gray whale one mile
down as leaf-cutter ants dismember
a nearby *guanacaste* and moths punish
the porchlight. Shoals of starlings
awash in a mackerel sky, small as
the rain that comes on in the distance.

III

Underwhelmed

Under the catastrophic dark,
the comet splintering the sky
with its ancient grief,
under the splay-handed palms,
under drinks glowering dark in
globes of glass, under the tender
humidity, the phosphorescent surf,
under the calls of nightjars
chuckling up from the ground,
under the ticking aloe under the moon's
absence, *under, under, under.*
Under the blinking stripes jets
write across the sky, under
stillness, the cabin pressure holding
steady, under the coned light
blanking out pages of gloss, under
the plunge of my love's hair, under
her sadness and her eyes
startling as stars, under our lives,
the miscarried child left in the bowl,
underground, underwater, understory,
under the bougainvillea's whorish musk,
under the coral's forest of horn, under
God, undertow, underdog, under
everything there is a season,
under the absence of twilight,
under the beach's grittle and bone,
under the words, startle, startle,
under the luxury of the table
so whitely laid, under
the candle's light shaped
like a hanging blade, we tear
apart the body of the fish and leave
glistening ladders of bone.

Quo Vadis?

. . . when you are old you will stretch out your hands, and another will gird you and take you where you do not want to go.
—John 21:18-19

The woman with the invisible stigmata
sits day by day in the *gelateria* and wonders
why no one else can see what she cannot,

though she knows her hands are carved
with holes, knows they are a blessing,
a punctured prompt that says suffering

is more than cars sizzling past in the drizzle,
history more than layered sediment in stone,
the tomb of a talking crow and Simon Peter

running from his execution. *Quo vadis?* he asks
the risen Lord who passes. When the answer
is a return to Rome and a second crucifixion,

Peter turns back to find his own death upside down.
Such stories are not to be trusted, she thinks.
Who asks for such a thing? A string of pain to tie

your eyes to. Eye your ties to, says the crow.
The rain keeps coming and the city has gone quiet.
The woman with the invisible stigmata hears

the crow call her name. She palms napkins stained
with flames of *mora e cioccolato* as men in black
waiting out the storm beneath the awning

pass their flat wit back and forth like cigarettes.
Children heave themselves into the rain.
A bouquet of umbrellas blossoms from their hands.

for Tony & Penelope

El Señor de los Temblores

Cuzco, Peru

That Christ is dark from candle black
comes as no surprise. The perfection

of his crucifixion carved into the whorls
and loops and ridges of his cross

paints the fingerprints of God on the wood
and electric votives turn a burned light

upon his dormancy. Even the crimson wig
of *ñucchu* flowers he wears—odd, fuschia curls

on the sagging head—hardly shocks;
such artifice unfolds throughout

this cathedral, miraculous anthill of gilt
and carving. In 1650, the Inca

still hiding in the towering green canyons,
He stopped the rolling pitch-pole earth

as the low arroyos shed their skins
and brimmed with sudden stone. The tremor

faded with the parade across the square,
el Señor held high above the quaking crowd

as banners of cloud assembled in glory
on the ridgelines. The spectacle

that calmed the earth, his hatchet face and
black plaited beard, the terrible need

of the gathering crowd: all this conspires
towards belief. That's what the painting

sharing the sacristy argues for; *el dios
herido* strokes the roaring earth with clouds,

beds it back down in blankets of sun.
Celebration rises up like a chorus of doves

from the crowd assembled in the square.
Easy to say that such faith is nothing

more than timing (the holy fathers offering up
their statuary in a fluke, the lofty trifecta

behind the altar glowing with the candelabra
of coincidence) but that would be to ignore

the river that flipped its banks and emptied
an agave field colonized by rats. That would be

to ignore the walls topped with *San Pedro* cactus
that collapsed in on a farmer and his wife as each prayed

for the death of the other, adobe bricks returning, *como
toda la carne*, to the earth from which they were made.

Landscape with Pigeons and the Tree of Heaven

When the sun skates behind the spire of the cathedral,
When that shadow paints a finger across the square where
      the flower vendor with daffodils in buckets sits
      in the new dark beneath the awning of the bank,
When the cars pause and the human traffic spills and gathers
      as oil above flame's blue petals buoying the black edges
      of a sauté pan,
When a woman passes flashing the sudden springtime
      of her thighs beneath kick pleats and piping,
When the world seems elegant and wet with promise,
      a corona of fire painted around the spire
      and tombstone arches of light from the bell tower
      paved into the square,
And, equally, when the sentimental gloss of sunlight is called
      into question by its absence,
When newspapers menace the fence as construction rumbles
      tectonically beyond the black-plastic sheeting,
And the grimy mitts of feral pigeons (*Columba livia*) chortle
      and bob their puffed, oiled iridescence beneath
      the ailanthus, chased by children with handfuls of corn,
I am reminded that in Chinese the ailanthus is the Tree
      of Heaven and pigeons are called the *clumsy bird*,
      relative of the dodo and other flightless doves
      extinct on islands across the Pacific,
I am reminded that the birds are symbol, the spirit in flames
      descending on the head of Christ, counterpart
      to the water of desire John drizzled upon his head,
I am reminded, too, that lovers should refrain from their consumption
      (said Martial, *Who would be lusty should not eat this bird*)
And that when Christ finally drove the traders from the temple,
      pigeons rose off the tables and swept the sky clean
      with their wings.

Landscape with Footnotes

---

1. A species of Amazonian bee that makes a remarkable, cylindrical hive. If disturbed, the bees will attack by stripping every hair from your body.
2. Bushmasters are the only snakes said to pursue people aggressively (although the fer-de-lance's venom is so powerful it once killed a woman tending the snakebite her husband had received).
3. Basilisks, or Jesus Christ Lizards, have large hind feet with flaps of skin between each toe. They move quickly across streams, aided by their web-like feet, which gives them the appearance of "walking on water."
4. *Dios te dé!* The Spanish for the toucan's call translates, "God keep you!"
5. The hoatzin is an ancient bird, an avian coelacanth; its young still possess claws on their wings.
6. Studies have shown that men are more content when the hierarchy between them and their compatriots is clear and well-established, even if they hold a low position in the hierarchy.

7. The bright crimson chest of the Resplendent Quetzal is a result, the story goes, of their empathy. After a battle between the Mayans and the Spanish conquistadors, Quetzals descended onto the battlefield and wept over the bodies of the dead Mayan soldiers. Their chests carry the color of the soldier's blood in remembrance.

8. Chambria palms carry seeds that are often infested with large, meaty grubs that taste like condensed milk.

9. The stilt palm, also called the walking palm, is said to walk to water during drought using its long skirt of roots.

10. The exact lines from Bishop:
    islands spawning islands,
    like frogs' eggs turning into polliwogs
    of islands, knowing that I had to live
    on each and every one, eventually,
    for ages, registering their flora,
    their fauna, their geography.

11. *Retama amarillo,* or "Spanish Broom," fills the *Valle Sagrado de Urubamba* that leads from Cuzco down to Machu Picchu and ultimately into the Amazon basin. Likewise, *el Rio Urubamba* connects the two halves of this story as we climb from the rainforest into the Andes.

12. *Los Incas* drank mainly *chicha* made from a fermentation of masticated corn. Only women chewed the corn. Legend has it that the prettier the girl, the better tasting the *chicha*.

13. The Yagua Indians paint their faces with the crushed seeds of the achiote—smeared on the skin it turns the color of oily paprika.

14. Inca is a dual use term—referring to both the people and their leader, *the Inca*.

15. Before Pizarro imprisoned the Inca, Atahualpa, they dined together often. Once when Atahualpa dropped some food on his clothing, he immediately got up to change. Pedro Pizarro (Francisco's cousin) asked him what the material was. "The finest hair of vampire bats," was the answer.

   "Where do you get so many?" Pizarro asked.

   "What else do those dogs of Tumbey and Puerto Viejo have to do," Atahualpa replied, "but capture such animals as to make clothes for me?" These clothes, like all the Inca's, were worn only once, then destroyed yearly in a special ceremony.

   Pizarro eventually had Atahualpa garroted and burned.

   Pizarro was killed himself in 1541, by Spaniards with whom he had conquered Peru and then betrayed.

   Church documents from the verification process for the remains of St. Toribio in 1661 note a wooden box inside of which was a lead box inscribed in Spanish: *Here is the skull of the Marquis Don Francisco Pizarro who discovered and won Peru and placed it under the crown of Castile.*

Landscape with Fig Trees and Strangulation

The streets of Beverly Hills colonnade
with ficus, smoothed-flanked, silver-barked allées

patched with black in the drizzle
of a wet January, but the strangler fig

arrives as shit in the cloud forest canopy
where a groove-billed ani spatters the bark

of an almond with its salt-and-pepper plaster.
Like *Philodendron panduraeforme,*

that horse-headed houseplant, it kicks out
aerial roots and lives on sunlight and dust,

the afternoon rain. Skin thin the roots drop.
Grimed with moss by the time they hit the floor

(double-helixed monkey ladders), they balloon
and round and ring; they shutter the almond

in buttresses of arch and wing. The fig
strangles the rotted, pipe-hollow parent.

In Spanish it's *el matapalo,* the killing tree—
its leaves hang on long petioles,

tincture of which both causes and cures
hemorrhage. It's Adam and Eve's tree

in the Garden of Eden,
source and cover for their shame,

and the bodhi where the Buddha
rested in the shade and was surprised

by nirvana in the washed-out sky.
The turning ellipticals of its leaves

sweep down in a wreckage of his past lives—
the son that he abandoned, the wife he left wet

in bed (*how bitter and sweet the two-toned flute of eros,*
how hollow at the core)—that sacred tree now decked

with oranges and wishes in a corral outside of Bodh Gaya.

Corcovado

Pelicans drop in tight as the waves pile up,
wingtips turned down to ride the swell

of air each wave pushes before it as it rises—
wingtips grazing water—rainforest hot

and raucous with the chatter of scarlet macaws
in the wild almond, and we walked the long thread

of sand out from camp, your eyes like the promise
of the wind taking the edge off the day's heat

and your skin iridescent in the light pitched
off the water, waves foaming beneath the moon

and slamming into the sand. Roar and then
the sudden silence. We walked and watched

the aureole of the moon smolder through clouds,
palm fronds snapping in the wind, we walked

with what is unspoken filling in our steps,
and in every gesture I saw you riding my hips,

clothes in a hoop around us, your small breasts,
your head back to the star-flowered sky.

Beauty's a theater of risk: heliconia flowers dangle
like orange rungs in the banana-leaved understory

and gesture to the hummingbirds whose throats flash
to catch the eye in the welter of the underbrush

where the ardor of the flowers—I have to touch myself
as I write this, pleasure rising like surf, the urge and thrust

of it heaping up and over and crashing onto the sand—
perfectly disguises the saffron coil of an eyelash viper.

Landscape with Dry Forest and Jack Gilbert

The hills above the veranda delight
in their dryness, their deprivation—
horse-poisonous *zarcilla* and the *guayacan*

roots roping limestone, sweet purple
fruits of the well-named dildo cactus
and the melon, thick phallus of thorn.

The scald of the noon sun and grackles
up the agave thickets. Every now
and again the scent of something dead

on the wind. Jack Gilbert whispers to me,
Deprivation is cultivation and the pounding
sun. That lunar ruin's a wealth unsurprises,

but in the red-veined shade of the sea grape,
your breasts are bare and white as night
flowers and you look at me with the hunger

of mistletoe reaching roots into drybark oak—
desire's delicacy and poison. Bullfinches
store scarcity in old cactus stems, and

the day becomes lavish with wind that wanders
into the sea-blight and emerges in a gust
of grasshoppers. Jack Gilbert crawls around

on the floor, searching for his wife's hair,
as the leaves of the *campeche* straighten
and rise in the heat that comes and comes on.

IV

Blind Desire

1.

The *O* as in an open door, the *I will be there.*
Vanity, vanity. The circling around,
as in absence (in Latin it's *from the stars*).

A feathered harp of winter sumac strummed
by water along the flooded river. A walkway
damp with fog, stairs that climb until they vanish.

Roads bustle with absent traffic, the mutter of all
conversations that have yet to happen, two
bodies cinched together at the gluttonous mouth.

2.

Two bodies woven into a twisted
biography of trees. Creepers and trunks,
the sudden canary fire of forsythia

blazing up hillsides. The birdhouse stuffed
with wire, mud, and grass. The whinny
of the robins above the whiskey-

scented mulch. The landscape collapses
into limbs. Spring leaves lie down,
small hands stroking the grass.

3.

Summer's leafy design dismantled
by a week's chill rain to a damp thatch
beneath the trees. She has vanished

up the stairs to sleep as the house creaks
in the cold stink of the wind—waiting
for the snow to come, waiting for its gargantuan

quiet to fall upon my life. The tv buzzing
technicolor: beer bottles, dead soldiers,
the found poem of the silver moon.

4.

A winter moon hung in the daylight sky.
The back cove. Three miles in twenty minutes,
breath like the body itself frothing out before me.

The tide pulls out and a bright wind blows in-
land, a scum of ice cauliflowered in the water.
Black backs and eider ducks rock in rafts

upon the water. The sun wets the limestone
on the path it touches and my love lies and lies
in a corridor of firelight stroking her hair.

5.

Her hair, the cleft of his mouth,
the arc of her breast, stiff tension
in the loins—two bodies

working together in the moon–
striped dark. The traffic that passes
paints a strange geometry

across the ceiling, their eyes closed
to the light of such terrible pleasure.
Pleasure. Then the falling away.

6.

Fog on the river falling away, the spillway
smoothed over. Blue tarps tent the bank.
Empty dock pilings spike the water where

the flood ripped boats from their cleats
and the planks from their pilings.
The river sediments a stratum of loss

along the bank, plastic like raffia plaited
through the trees. All the world in flux:
the heart a hatbox full of eels.

7.

Fairy houses of stick and bark, hatbox
and four-square, toy-subdivision
frosted nacreous with mussel shells.

Death-head juniper berries, tiny geography
of hope blocked out across a pine-streaked
half-acre. Alone on the scraped granite

shore—she's gone. The wind-sculpted
spruce and black oak semaphore offshore.
The cold ocean, the sculpted world.

8.

A sculpture of gulls on the tarmac, heads
pinned against the wind, the cold light
gray as the cloudcover that drapes

the russet hills. Spring begins
in the smallest argument of green. Desire
follows and what it feeds on, flush as the water

over the spillway, the foursquare skeleton
of the steelworks rust-blasted below
the overpass and the sky, battered open.

9.

The sky as red as rose-tinged flesh,
like sex-flushed skin, the chestnut broken
beneath my boot. The lilac thrums

with hummingbirds blazing into flight,
a hillside orchard of inedible apples.
Dawn-blushed peaches rot on the ground.

Dusk lights up the hills along the river,
clouds lit like snowcover above. Laughter
from the open mouths of other people's houses.

10.

The mouths of the blooming
trees, a warm wind comes down,
the brown earth rapt with petals,

thin skin of henna. Rain avenues
down from the asphalt sky, glitters
like galaxies in the grass.

Beware, Josephine, wrote Napoleon,
beware. One fine night the door
will be broken down and I will be there.

V

Ars Poetica with Pain

In this one, Yosemite Sam gets hung. Bugs digs
his way into the prison yard after he missed

that mythical left at Albuquerque and soon Sam's big hat flaps
in the wind, his knee-high, shitkickers jerking in midair.

It's not Eurydice stumbling into ecstasy up the moss-
tumbled steps, Orpheus erect before her;

it's not Bugs smacking carrots as the fade circles down
around him and the cursive loops across the screen—

craft and the hero victorious in the common tongue.
All the strange grammars of success yield

the elastic cat who balloons back to wholeness
after being smacked with the frying pan,

or the duck that slips his bill back across his jaw
after eating a load of buckshot. Never the scene

when Elmer Fudd blotches his crotch with piss
when Bugs readies to take his kneecaps

with his own shotgun. In this one, Eurydice
chews on a worm of pain that sounds like *farewell*

to Orpheus, untuned to the choral music of Hell
and Orpheus' head, cast aside, floats forever singing.

In this one, the Thracian women toss the broken lyre,
mangled as a smashed racket, into the fire and smile

as smoke ropes up around their throats
and the strings hiss and curl into ampersands.

Stalin on Stage

The angelic gilt of the ceiling lit
with stage-light imitation, fractured
surf of the gold leaf pouring across
the proscenium, the aging rafters,
the crowd speckled with reflection:
all this brings us to Stalin.
Stalin on stage. To the moment
when he has just finished speaking
and the audience rises in unison
to collapse the air with their applause.
Minutes pass and no one will stop,
the very air threatened by the noise,
until one general, veteran of wars
and Tannenberg, an armada
of ribbons blockading the deep Baltic
of his uniform, drops his hands and sits.
We know the history so we know
the story now, before it's given.
How he is rousted and pummeled
at dawn and the trees in a cold grove
gather round him as the rifles rise.
Never be the first to stop applauding Stalin,
he is told, before the guns' ovation
rises up into the glacial sky, birdcall
returning after a brief silence. This
is wrong, as I return to the source
to reread the history, the general just
an owner, his paper factory offering up
the forms that will be filled out to detail
the reams of his misfortune. He wasn't
killed, wasn't turned out into the morning
trees and introduced to the tiny mouths
of twenty weapons. He was given ten
years in the gulag, ten years at labor
in the flesh-splitting cold, ten years
in the joy of short sunlight. *Ten years.*
Does that make it better or worse?

On his release, his daughter's there
to collect him, and they hobble into
the flat March light, holding on to
each other in the Riga station.

The train pulls at them as it leaves,
the sound of its wheels on the ties
at the crossing like men beating a horse
with boards. The train that once
carried the poem's moral center
vanishes into a cold drizzle that falls
on their necks, gilds their hair with dew
the hue of piss, almost the color
of the wash of gold above Stalin,
who remains, of course, up on stage
beneath the clarion lights and seraphs,
his face bright as paper, drenched
in the warmth of the applause
that somehow never dies.

Before Trinity

a conflagration that would overturn
the palace of the sky

—Ovid

In white sands anchored by sage
and ocotillo, a cactus wren,

its small black eye a small black world
burning, alights and doesn't know its life

counts only minutes now before it turns
to a puff a jellied fire. The woman

navigating the canyons beyond *Ojo Caliente*,
headlights draped across the pendular hills,

kids slapped across the backseat,
senses none of this as static overtakes her radio

and her horn-rims reflect a tiny brightness
past the horizon. She's been driving all night,

the silver silo of coffee thrust between her thighs.
She doesn't know safety's a matter of the odds

now that the world's been made that much more
savage. In hours her children will wake

and stretch with stupid, sleep-filled mouths
and gape at the dry washes and sagey hillsides,

the land stunned with sunlight. The boys
will stagger off to piss in the clean dawn,

thin streams of gold wire tying them
to the earth, and they will barely feel

the small finery of ash that lands on
their eyelashes and dusts their faces like wings.

Amazon Parable

The bees that will strip every hair
from your head instead of swelling
your hands with a thatch of venom,

that will leave you bald and clean
and unstung, they are my subject
today. Whether this hive, cylindrical

and birchy, lie or not, the shape of threat
that hangs above the white river
south of Iquitos in the meandering fan

of the Tahuayo, whether this hive houses
such hazard can't matter. The story carries
its own weight, as does the ass that carried

Christ off the Mount of Olives,
its sweat-worked back, the rope-burn
that pinks its muzzle. It stands

beneath the awful sun as the pigeons
explode from the temple in a flaring
of white wings and slapping. But this

was never about the ass, really, or the fig tree
withered beneath the hand but the weight
the story carries—told in the boat as we

thrum upriver—the strange menace of power,
the shearing leaving you stripped
to flushed flesh beneath gaudy palms
ticking above, fanning you, blessing you.

L&scape with Cause & Effect

Because in a box canyon below *Cerro
de la Meurte*, where *el Rio Savegre*
cuts through rolled boulders & plashes
clear as acrylic in plunge pools, where
hummingbirds slash & chip niches out
of hyacinth & orchid, small orchards,
the dry oak forest knotted & hung
with bromeliads, clouds & sky,

& because of the Talamanca range, abrupt
out of the Pacific, clouds lave the canyons,
the forests, the air verdant & chiming
with water from every pitched boulder
& tree ferns prehistoric in the under-
story. Because philodendron leaves
like slotted spoons skulk up buttressed
trunks in the canyons of the Resplendent
Quetzal, & because the male launches
from the crowns, circles in song & rockets

down, because Quetzal tail feathers
parse the moment of creation & the will
of the creator's sine-flight through the light-
sliced noon, emerald streamers gone gold,
because of their crimson chests,

                     & because, *there*,
after ten years of trails staircased through
roots of brazilletto & oak, ten years of DEET
& sweat, stoic in the branches, the black
bead of his eye, *he's there*, & then because
two females retreat & twist through layers
of the cloud forest (his tail serpentine behind
him like a caduceus) the male follows.

The Blue Dolphin

Oh, but it is dirty!
—Elizabeth Bishop

Above the wrack line where the beach lips
up

and the wind has been working all day with
gulls

and clouds coming up out of the east,
their

trumpeting joy in the rowdy fields of
the sky,

the bloated body of a bottlenose
tossed

by the last tide
rots.

Eyes excavated from the humped head
and

odd hieroglyphics runneled
into

the blackening rubber body,
it's lost

any beauty it once laid claim to.
Still,

someone has painted the dolphin blue,
a cerulean

matched to the patch of sky that has
lingered

on the horizon since sunrise.
Someone

worked the nozzle over the body,
careful

to leave no sign of how what was done
was done.

When the Park Service truck cleans the
carcass

off the beach nothing remains, but
the wind

runs the sand and the black
wrack

of seaweed. Still someone took her
time,

someone loved this black sack of hide just
enough

to make a blue hole in the sand.

Landscape with Escaped Ostriches

1.

If, in Wisconsin, rounding the corner near Little Sand, a slice of lake
notched between stiletto pines, the grubby, swan-winged sacks

racing at the fence, the two-toed ridiculousness
of the ostriches doesn't drive you off the road into a suddenly
    silent ditch—

their plucky stares as you approach the electric fence from the
    unwrecked car,
dirty snowball bodies carried on legs all sinew and angle, spurs ready

to rip a cable of muscle from your thigh, the slouch of barns
behind them—when you are asked to describe this later

2.

over drinks in the knotty pine bar, northwoods kitsch nicking out
from every corner like stuffed wolverines,

flightless ratites, you can say, birds with flat breastbones lacking keels for
the muscles that power flight. (From the Latin *ratites*, marked with the
    figure of a raft.)

> [Under **raft**, *n*, see no. 3: an aggregation of animals (as waterfowl)
> resting on the water.]

Say *Struthio camelus*, the camel (footed) ostrich—like the Vorompatra or
    elephant bird,
9 ft extinct flightless fructivore of Madagascar—

presently the largest of existing birds.

3.

You can also say ostrich eyes are largest (per body size) of any animal.
    Their arch
and bulge leaves little room for a brain;

thus the ostrich pecks repeatedly at the glinty sticker on the car window,
    then swallows
the nothing she has consumed.

4.

Say how, in the 1870s, it was suddenly fashionable for ladies to be seen
with a feather boa or a sarong made from enormous feathers

so, in Little Karoo, Oudtshoorn alone, farmers exported 450,000
kilograms of feathers per year.

*The wings of the ostrich wave proudly; but are they the feathers and plumage
    of love?*
asks the Book of Job. It is a rhetorical question.

5.

And there's more to tell, how ostriches have been known to
    direct courtship
behavior at humans—the amorous male sinks down on his haunches,
        swaying from side to side,

how in South Africa, ostriches have been trained as shepherds,
    running rings
around skittish sheep beneath the camel-skinned hills.

The ostrich, says Job, *scorneth the horse and his rider.*

In Egypt, ostriches were once hitched to chariots,
but the birds ran in circles,

6.

and so the practice abandoned,

7.

but save the story of Sidi Mohamed for last. That boy of six
  who wandered
off a hardpan plantation and stepped into a vault of bullhorn acacia,
  gamba tussocks,

the ginormous sky

where he met the ostriches who adopted him. Until he was captured
by hunters ten years later, he lived on grass.

I have become a brother to the jackals, and go about in the company of ostriches.

8.

Here the story calls for your embellishment (by this time you'll be on
your second round, tawny glasses spoked with light from the late sun)

as the boy's language was a chucking hiss, a ululating warble
  never deciphered,
his body glazed with feathers, guano beneath his nails when the dogs
  pinned him
up a tree.

9.

That's the problem with such stories; they wander off sometimes
under huge skies and never find their way home.

You have to struggle out after them with dogs and lunch,
resting in whatever shade you find. The dogs

are exhausted, their long tongues lolling in the dirt, a tempest of
  flies whirling
around their eyes. So, eat the meat you've brought and finish the water.

Lay the shotgun across your elbow like a lover's arm.

When we have passed the hour of the hottest sun we'll set out again, each step leading us ceaselessly toward that homey clutch

of birds gathering together at the horizon.